SPECTRUM® READERS

LEVEL 1

LET'S GO!
Visit the Zoo

By Lisa Kurkov

 Carson-Dellosa Publishing

An imprint of Carson-Dellosa Publishing, LLC
P.O. Box 35665
Greensboro, NC 27425-5665

carsondellosa.com

Printed in the USA. All rights reserved.
ISBN 978-1-4838-0113-1

01-002141120

Today, we are
visiting the zoo.
Let's go see
the animals!

Otter

Let's watch the otter
swim and play.
Otters use rocks to
open shells.

Penguin

Let's watch penguins
dive and swim.
Penguins are birds,
but they cannot fly.

Octopus

Let's touch the
tentacles of an
octopus.
An octopus can
swim backward!

Sea Lion

Let's visit sea lions
lying on a rock.
Mother sea lions
nurse their babies
for over a year.

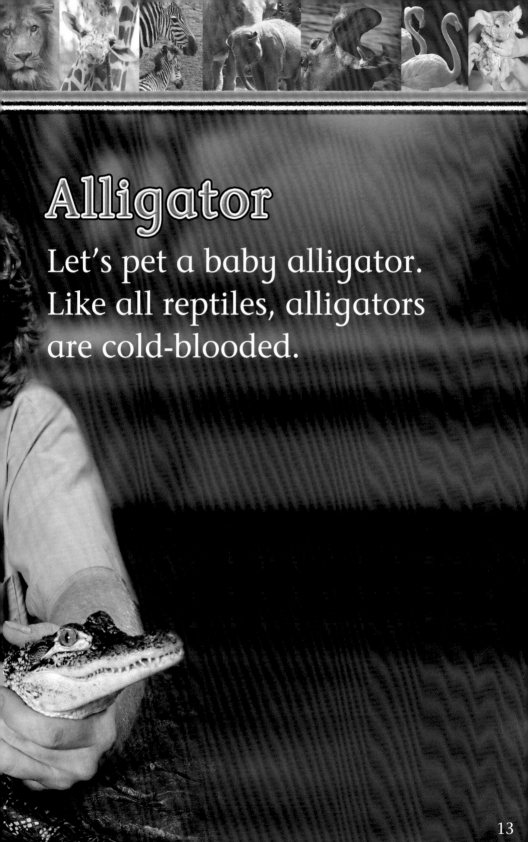

Alligator

Let's pet a baby alligator. Like all reptiles, alligators are cold-blooded.

Snake

Let's touch a
milk snake's
smooth scales.
This snake is
not poisonous.

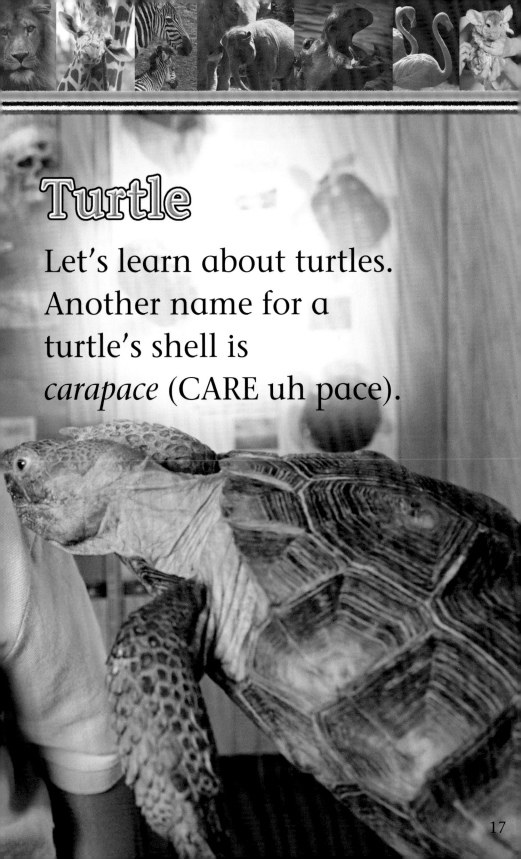

Turtle

Let's learn about turtles.
Another name for a
turtle's shell is
carapace (CARE uh pace).

Lion

Let's visit an
African lion.
Only male lions
have manes.

Giraffe

Let's look up to see the tall giraffes. They can be three times as tall as an adult human.

Zebra

Let's watch zebras
trot on their hooves.
No two zebras have
the same stripes.

Elephant

Let's visit African
elephants.
To stay cool, they
flap their big ears
and spray water.

Hippo

Let's listen to a
hippo roar.
Hippos cannot
swim, but they like
to walk in rivers.

Flamingo

Let's watch a flamingo stand on one leg. Flamingoes have pink feathers because they eat pink shrimp!